Earth Soldier Evolution

The Poetic Critique of an Athlete's Imagination

By Don "Poncho" Robinson

Earth Soldier Evolution: The Poetic Critique of an Athlete's Imagination

athleticalchemy.com

In conjuction with
earthsoldierlifestyle.com
blackpeopledata.com

By Don Robinson Copyright @ 2025

ISBN: 978-0-9826994-4-7

All rights reserved. No parts of this book may be reproduced in any form without permission in writing from the publisher, except by a reviewer who may quote brief passages for reviewing purposes.

Don Robinson is the author of the Earth Soldier Trilogy.

Earth Soldier: Relationships Define Our Purpose
Earth Soldier Unveiled: 13 The Transfer of AI Power
Earth Soldier Evolution: The Poetic Critique of an Athlete's Imagination

...OND NEWS LEADER, Thursday, October 5, 1989

Bruce Parker/The Richmond News Leader

After adjusting to new system, Donald Robinson's game is coming together.

It's a non-district game, but it's not just another game to Robinson.

"All my old friends that I played with for so many years, I finally get a chance to play against them," he said. "I'm gonna enjoy every minute of it."

Of the Springers, Robinson said split end David McLeod was probably his best friend. The two may well go head-to-head tomorrow night.

"This'll be the first time playing against him," Robinson said. "I'm looking forward to it. Friend on friend — no problem. We'll leave it all on the field."

As for his decision to leave Highland Springs, Robinson is firm.

"I'm enjoying it here," he said, smiling. "I don't regret it all."

Table of Contents

Chapter 1: Athletic Alchemy – The Seed of Growth 5

Chapter 2: Setting the Stage 11

Chapter 3: The Role of Faith, Philosophy, and Self-Discovery............16

Chapter 4: Transcendence – Beyond the Field 24

Chapter 5: The Soul of an Athlete...35

Chapter 6: Football Expanded My World View 39

Chapter 7: Critiqued Poems..45

Chapter 8: The Arena – Lessons Learned Through Competition.......68

"For man's entire life is determined by that figure, that dominant figure, that he holds in his Imagination. He believes himself to be this, that or the other, and it's going to influence his every action in the world. He can think that he's wanted or unwanted, wise or unwise. No matter what he thinks, that dominant figure will influence everything that he does. For man's true environment is really in his Imagination."

- Neville Goddard – May 14, 1963

Introduction

I loved it! Every week, spectators poured in, creating a vibrant community that extended from the open field at the end of our block to the neighborhood basketball court, or the football stadium. They left their troubles on the sidewalk or at the entrance to the arena, becoming part of something bigger. My older cousin took me on bike rides throughout the city to different African-American streetball hotspots in search of competition. He knew the level of competition in those redline neighborhoods was unmatched. It was asphalt, heat, aggression, and quick feet racing back and forth from sun up to sundown, and we were all part of it.

I also accompanied my dad to basketball courts around the city and county. He introduced me to the men who were wired for extreme competition. My desire to compete was forged in the Richmond city heat. I passed through Church Hill and Jackson Ward, once a political stronghold for black people in Richmond. The historical significance of these places, their role in shaping the community and the sport, coursed through me like a potent energy, connecting me to a rich past where communities thrived in athletics, politics, and culture.

Learning the rules of the courts with my dad at Hotchkiss Field on the north side and Dabbs House in Henrico was like a ritual of repeated competitive baptisms where the pulse of competition was so loud that if you didn't fight back, it snatched your breath away and left you standing defeated blocking the view of screaming spectators.

These competitive hotspots were more than just a collection of streets; they were a biological protein delivery system for athletic excellence, feeding the competitive spirit with ancestral energy. I stepped onto those courts not just to face the best athletes in the state but to be transformed by the unseen forces swirling in the air. Each jump shot, each defensive stance, and each bead of sweat was alchemy in motion, fusing history and competition to forge something entirely new within me. It was a journey of self-discovery and transformation that continues to inspire me to this day.

As athletes, we carry the legacy of our communities, of families who dared to hope and persevere. Every step, every win, is a tribute to their resilience. Let us align our actions with their dreams, and together, let's prove that true victory is a world where no odds are stacked against anyone. It's a responsibility we all share.

It became clear to me that sports were not just a hobby, but a powerful tool that led me on a transformative journey of self-discovery. My dad was a talented safety in high school. As I engaged in various athletic pursuits, I found myself peeling back the layers of my identity, gaining a better understanding of who I am and my place within the colorful dynamics of my community.

Off the field, this resilience is a call to honor our legacy by becoming more: more compassionate, more determined, and more attuned to the power within. Challenges test our will to survive, but they also ignite the fire to thrive. As athletes, we have the opportunity to let those experiences shape us into instruments of change, creating harmony between personal growth and our impact on the world. True victory is living aligned with that purpose.

Along this path, I found myself asking deep questions about the individuals who surrounded me, the intricate dynamics of my relationships, and our collective responsibility towards the world around us. Each inquiry acted as a significant milestone, guiding me through the twists and turns of my introspective journey.

As a young African American male, my journey was often marked by unique challenges that shaped my perspective and led me to seek the guidance necessary for my transition into manhood. The support and wisdom of my community were not just helpful, but indispensable, playing a pivotal role in shaping my understanding and helping me navigate this crucial chapter of my life. The real competition was not against others on the field, but a personal battle against my limitations, pushing me to reach new heights I never thought possible. I was an athlete because that was my only and best option to start.

Chapter 1
Athletic Alchemy – The Seed of Growth

Mom Childhood Dreams
"It wasn't just about winning—it was about discovering who I was beneath the uniform."

What role did my mom play? Well, she gave birth – need I say more?

My great-grandmother and maternal and paternal grandmother created a situation and environment to raise me in.

Their sacrifices and unwavering love created the foundation for every accomplishment I've achieved. My mother, the embodiment of their strength, instilled in me the drive to push beyond systemic hurdles, using my God-given talents to honor our family's resilience. Every step forward—on the court, in the classroom, or life—is a testament to the legacy of perseverance and determination passed down through generations. So, when she made the journey to watch me play in Montreal, her pride mirrored my own. It was a celebration, not just of the game, but of the extraordinary journey that brought us here. Once we arrived, we shared a few cold Canadian beers. I enthusiastically told her just how tasty Canadian beer was, and she nodded in agreement, her eyes sparkling with delight.

This trip marked a significant milestone for her; it was her first venture out of the country, and it was to offer support to her son on the field – a satisfying experience, to say the least. Reflecting on her life, I see a remarkable testament to strength and sacrifice. She became pregnant as a teenager, a testament to her strength, trading her youth for the warmth of motherhood and nurturing me through the formative years.

As I sit back and ponder the moments we could create together, I can't help but think about my grandmother. I imagine her pride in witnessing her first grandchild share such treasured moments with her daughter in a new land. Perhaps we were both experiencing something my grandmother had envisioned long ago, a dream she held for our family.

Imagination is the spark
Sometimes, the emotions evoked by an imagined experience can rival those of the actual event—imagination and reality work in harmony, like a lock fitting into its key. Imagination acts as the key that unlocks all the possibilities of experience. This book opened my eyes to the dynamic at play throughout my life; I can see how experiences unfold before me, and then I truly live and embrace them.

> **"Imagination is where every dream begins. Before you can run the race, make the play, or win the game, you have to see it in your mind. The power to visualize isn't just a skill—it's the key to unlocking what's possible." – Serena Williams**

Imagination is the spark born from any moment I visualize and create. It's the wellspring of endless possibilities, the essence of what it means to dream. Poetry is the action framework, the vessel I use to give form to the energy I generate through thought and imagination. It adds color, texture, and depth, transforming the intangible into something I can express and share. The energy becomes consciously accessible through poetry—words capturing moments, emotions, and ideas in their purest forms.

And then there's sports—the third state lends itself to physical manifestation. It's where the initial energy, thought, and moment takes full shape in the body, in movement, in action. Even with poetry, I capture a moment so vividly that I must focus entirely, immersing myself 100% in the present to reflect it truthfully in my writing. The creative force I tapped into when stepping into that flow state is realizing who I am – in the moment, acknowledging the powerful emotion supporting that realization, its relationship to a subject matter, and capturing it in all words.

Imagination, poetry, and sports formed a seamless cycle in my evolution: envisioning, shaping, and attempting to live each moment with clarity, passion, and purpose - while trying to remain grateful through the struggles.

They Planted it in me

Growing up, food was more than just sustenance; it was a means of feeling connected, grounded, and loved. I often fantasized about both of my grandmother's cooking—the warmth of their cornbread, the richness of their greens, and the joy those meals brought to our family table. Those memories became my haven, a place I would return to during stressful times. Food brought us together and made us feel connected. It wasn't just about filling your belly—it was about the love and the stories that came with every bite.

Food is not just calories or macros. It's alive. It's energy that can change how you feel, move, and connect with people. It's a part of who we are, whether you're sitting around a family table or prepping for a big game. That's why I can't look at food as just fuel. It's part of my story, culture, and journey as an athlete and a man. It's a part of my identity, and many of you can relate to this sentiment.

After one particularly tough high school game, a friend surprised me with a homemade cake. I hadn't even mentioned my craving for it, but it felt as if my thoughts had somehow reached the universe, and it delivered what I needed. That experience made me wonder: was my imagination more potent than I realized? My stomach answered, yes!

Key moments in athletic competition that shapes your character. "In the heat of competition, we face not only our opponents but also our deepest fears and aspirations."

There were times when the fear of failing had a firm grip on my emotions. I knew one slip would sometimes send hundreds or thousands of people into a frenzy of excitement while the other 20,000 on-lookers dropped their heads in disbelief. All of this happens in a matter of seconds. Regardless of the stakes, I step up to the line, take my position, control my breathing, and embrace the moment. I realize the strength is in facing the fear and not criticizing myself for feeling afraid.

Breaking One-Dimensional Stereotypes: Athletes are often seen solely as physical performers, but their imaginative and emotional depth highlights their complexity and humanity, elevating their societal image.

Bridging Creativity and Discipline: The ability to visualize and embrace experiences demonstrates how athletes embody both creative intuition and rigorous discipline, reshaping perceptions of their contributions beyond sports.

Expanding Inspirational Roles: By showcasing their multidimensional nature, athletes transcend traditional roles to become relatable figures who inspire personal and societal growth.

Challenging Traditional Narratives: Acknowledging the harmony between imagination and reality allows athletes to redefine their influence, proving they are innovators and thinkers, not just performers.

My earliest memory of playing organized football is walking to practice from 27th Street to old Armstrong High School and eating chocolate chip cookies my mom gave me. She worked at Nabisco at the time. The dreams I had then about playing on TV were in the mind of an eight-year-old. Sitting in the room with my football and watching games with my dad fed the desire. As an athlete rising through the ranks, the simplicity of specific dreams and desires remains while the difficulty of realizing those dreams skyrockets. The relationships in your life change, but your dreams stay the same. Protecting that dream becomes crucial for some of us as we compete against all the other good and bad distractions, such as injuries, personal issues, and societal pressures that an older, mature mind locks into. Sometimes, I wished for that simplicity surrounding my dream when I walked to practice eating chocolate chip cookies.

Athletics is more than competition; it is a mirror for life's greatest lessons. Each practice refines your skill, but each challenge shapes your character. Success on the field means nothing if it doesn't align with who you're becoming as a person.
The real game is within—how you honor your talents, push through limitations, and carry the lessons of teamwork and resilience into every facet of your life.

Chapter 2
Setting the Stage

"An athlete is more than strength and skill—they are a bridge between youthful dreams and mature reflection, constantly evolving and breaking stereotypes to embrace courage in the face of the unknown."

- **Other titles I contemplated:**
- "The Competitive Spirit: A Journey Through Growth"
- "Between the Lines: Sports and the Art of Becoming"

"Every game or journey begins with preparation, even if the road ahead remains unknown."

Personal evolution is the silent force shaping every athlete's journey, blending raw potential with hard-earned wisdom. Each challenge faced and milestone achieved becomes a lesson, revealing the layers of personality often hidden behind the stereotype of sheer physical prowess. This journey of self-discovery transforms the athlete into a multidimensional figure who learns to balance youthful dreams with the resilience and determination required to navigate life's complexities. The most profound lessons emerge within this evolution, inspiring personal growth and breaking barriers for others to follow.

High school to Hamilton
The team dynamics were familiar, but I was different. The picture of myself drinking water on the sidelines at my high school game, positioned with the photo of me playing in a CFL game, conveys this journey. Both on and off the field, growth is a journey of becoming. The team dynamics may feel familiar, and the plays might echo those you've run

before, but you are never the same person twice. The image of yourself as a young athlete—eager, learning, striving—holds the seed of who you are today. But the photo of you on the professional stage? That is the bloom of perseverance, discipline, and self-discovery.

At the time, it never made sense to me. The moments shared in this book were experienced by a different version of myself and, at times, disjointed when I experienced them in real-time, making it difficult for me to understand the unseen hand, creating an ark of experiences. Many of these experiences were impossible to foresee. Adopting the persona of an athlete is no different from embracing any other identity—it can inflate the ego and limit personal growth in areas that don't directly support that role. For example, while writing poetry didn't improve my athletic performance, it was essential to shaping my worldview and personal development beyond sports.

Any title or identity we take on has the potential to both preserve and restrict certain aspects of our personality. This can be a double-edged sword, keeping us focused and hindering growth. If we become too attached to one role, we risk being unprepared when life inevitably changes.

My 18-year journey in organized sports was deeply personal, marked by both growth and stagnation. This book reflects that journey, connecting different experiences to illustrate a clear and steady evolution. It condenses the transition from childhood to adulthood into just a few pages, each experience serving as a testament to the intricate nature of change and its expression in our lives over time.

A freshman

I was cut from my middle school football team in the sixth grade—the fate of a freshman. Two years later, I played varsity football in high school as a freshman. Four years later I played one of my first games on television at the University of Tennessee. At that time, I was a freshman cornerback for the University of Kentucky. The stadium was packed and so loud that I couldn't hear the defensive back standing beside me. I was one of two freshmen defending two of the best receivers in the SEC, which was happening on national television.

This odyssey of self-discovery reshapes the athlete into a richly multidimensional figure who learns to harmonize their youthful aspirations with the unwavering resilience and determination required to navigate the intricate complexities of life. Through this transformative evolution, the most significant lessons emerge, inspiring personal growth, paving the way for others, dismantling barriers, and setting new precedents for those who aspire to follow.

I've come to realize that it's not only acceptable but also invigorating to approach new challenges with the curiosity and resilience of a freshman. I cultivate a habit of bravery by intentionally placing myself in situations that stretch my comfort zone. Each experience, whether daunting or exhilarating, adds to my reservoir of courage, making it easier for me to rise to the occasion when it truly matters. Indeed, stepping into the unfamiliar realm requires a bold heart.

A Relic

Maybe you, like me, are a relic being passed down through generations, each carrying a piece of our family's legacy. Living with all three grandmothers, I absorbed some of their wisdom, each one burying a precious nugget of knowledge within me. Their life principles, so easily understandable even for a child, became our guiding light. Like a strong adhesive, these principles bound our family dynamics to my grandmother's vision for future generations.

The Principles they taught served as mathematical equations expressing the value of positive self-expression and community support. The techniques these matriarchs taught were steeped in belief and self-actualization principles that generated energy. I could use this energy in other parts of my life. My grandmothers spoke about strategies for survival in the sweetest way. Maybe they slice the first piece of a freshly baked pie, and as their hands push it across the table towards me, they smile and ask, "You remember why it's important to treat people like you would want to be treated, right?" Looking back, I probably thought I wouldn't want to deny anybody the experience I was about to have with this pie. Of course, the more profound reflections came after digesting the pie.

Like an alchemist, I was able to transform those teachings into a different form of self-expression. My dad, a pivotal figure in my personal growth journey, taught me how to use my body with the energy generated from my grandmother's lessons. He instilled in me the belief that the alignment of the mind and body is the key to reaching a state of flow with the potential to outperform the opponent. My ability to fully immerse myself in the moment was a gift handed down to me. Each desire was a practice in feeling the wish fulfilled, a sensory explosion of food, play, or time with family and friends, born first in my imagination and then experienced.

Chapter 3
The Role of Faith, Philosophy, and Self-Discovery

The interplay of faith, spirituality, and metaphysics in shaping your perspective as both an athlete and a person. Athleticism tests the body, but it's the spirit that carries us forward.

Shooting a jump shot: Visualizing Victory
"An athlete isn't just defined by their physical abilities but by the depth of their values, emotions, and convictions. Breaking stereotypes, they can embody emotional intelligence, faith, and purpose while still excelling in their sport."

The exchanges with family members, rich with wisdom and resilience, gave me the tools to see beyond the surface. They helped me understand that the challenges we faced weren't just personal but part of a larger narrative—one rooted in histories of injustice but also in the relentless pursuit of dignity and equity.

My paternal grandmother followed the Apostolic Pentecostal Church faith, and her influence on me was fundamental. She was a pillar of strength and faith in our family, and I was drawn to the same beliefs. From sun up to sun down on Saturday, we didn't participate in activities other than church service and family gatherings, where we discussed weekly events and shared a meal. We recognized and honored the Sabbath, a tradition my grandmother instilled in me. Because of my faith, I would arrive at games late on Saturdays. I thought nothing of it as a child. I don't even remember how my teammates felt about it. It must have been strange for a starting athlete to place his faith above athletics.

Maybe the experience gave me perspective, even though I was unaware then.

Basketball, I learned, is not just a physical game—it's a mental one too. Before every competition, I would immerse myself in a mental rehearsal, picturing myself on the court: the perfect crossover, the defender stumbling back, the clean arc of the ball as it swished through

During those impressionable preteen years, I realized that growth wasn't just about achievements but the spaces and conversations that shaped my world perception. My neighborhood, sports programs, schools, and church were more than just settings—they were crucibles where my values were forged.

As athletes, we carry the lessons of these formative years onto the field, but our true victory lies in aligning that growth with who we become beyond the game. We transform ourselves and the systems and communities we touch by honoring those early lessons.

the net. I visualized it so vividly that, during games, it felt like muscle memory, as though I was living something I had already practiced a thousand times in my mind. This realization was a game-changer for me—imagination isn't just daydreaming; it's preparation. Every shot I visualized seemed to bring me closer to making it a reality.

It wasn't magic, but it felt like alignment, like seeing the future I wanted and stepping into it like my faith and actions were in sync. This understanding of the power of visualization in my performance was not just a revelation but a source of inspiration and motivation that I carry with me to this day.

Respect for Principles: Redefining Success Metrics

Challenge: Choosing faith over team obligations can cause friction with peers.

Opportunity: Demonstrate how steadfast adherence to principles earns respect and sets an example of integrity.

Challenge: Society often values athletic achievement above personal beliefs or emotional depth.

Opportunity: Show how a multidimensional approach leads to balanced, holistic success, both on and off the field.

The Line We Cross: Competition and Camaraderie

Each line marks a growth and transition. I bend my knees, touching the first line. I'm aware of the eventual pain that will sit in. The burning sensation is in my mind first. The second line came much quicker than I expected, but I wanted to be first. My breathing isn't easy, and I must keep my thoughts busy. Thinking about the pain before it arrives is a distraction and sometimes makes you dizzy. That third line got me thinking about the fourth. I want to get in shape. I want to win. I feel it in my stomach. Each line I cross, I win, but this is just the first suicide.

My coach is saying things to keep us in the moment. He is telling us to think about what we have to do now – in the NOW.

"Pick up your legs," – he said as his voice ricocheted off the bouncing ball sound. He wants us to think only about how deep we must go to perform in the now. Each of us heard his voice, but the experience brought us closer, not the sound of the whistle or the clapping hands. We were all Crossing the Line together while we ran.

I finished the first suicide. While we stand awaiting the whistle, I look over at my teammates. We experience that hurt and pain together. But when I'm in the moment – it's just me. I see the lines and anticipate having to do all three. It felt like my coach was looking directly at me. I realized that crossing the line meant overcoming these burdensome thoughts. Ignoring the pain that hadn't happened, stop making assumptions about the others enduring the discomfort with me. Each realization felt like I was crossing a line. Toward the end of the third suicide, the pain wasn't hard to find—no need to expect pain in my mind. My teammates and I encouraged each other to pass the time. Hundreds of these experiences have helped bind and refine our commitment to Crossing the Line.

I jump High
It's time to celebrate

I imagined flying high to the basketball rim. I imagined jumping over the high jump bar. I broke my middle school high Jump record, a feat that symbolized my dedication and love for the feeling of leaping into flight. I leaped 7'0, cleared the bar, and was so excited – I couldn't wait to hit the high jump mat. I raised my head to watch my ankles clear the bar, and my ankles dropped, brushing the bar off to the ground. Discipline Donald, what happened to your discipline? Keep your head back, and your ankles will rise. I wanted to see the manifestations born from my imagination take on the clothes of reality in real time. I can hear my jump coaches, Coach Spain and Coach Robinson say – "discipline, be patient."

"An athlete's imagination fuels more than physical achievements—it embodies emotional intelligence, discipline, and the ability to visualize success beyond limitations, breaking stereotypes and elevating the human experience."

1. **Athlete as a Visionary**
   - **Challenge:** Athletes are often seen as purely physical performers.
   - **Opportunity:** An ability to visualize, strategize, and manifest success, proving mental acuity and creativity.

2. **Emotional Depth and Reflection**
   - **Challenge:** Society may overlook the emotional intelligence required for self-assessment and growth.
   - **Opportunity:** Highlight the introspection athletes engage in to refine their craft, inspiring others to value self-improvement.

3. **Breaking the "Physical-Only" Stereotype**
   - **Challenge:** Athletes are stereotyped as individuals who succeed solely due to natural talent or physical prowess.
   - **Opportunity:** Share stories that reveal their dedication, focus, and emotional resilience as integral components of their success.

4. **Rewriting Societal Narratives**
   - **Challenge:** The social perception often limits athletes to a single dimension of fame or skill.
   - **Opportunity:** Athletes are multi-faceted individuals whose journey combines imagination, discipline, and determination, inspiring a broader definition of success.

The Traveler: Two Sports In College

Traveling from university to university for games laid a foundation I wasn't consciously aware of at the time - traveling. I've always had an active imagination and often envisioned myself traveling and experiencing different places, but I didn't have access to make those dreams a reality. Suddenly, as part of a team in the Southeastern Conference, I flew to different universities, stepped into new environments, and broadened my horizons.

As a dual-sport athlete, my involvement in track and field added another layer to these experiences. Transitioning to track during the off-season protected my body from the grueling toll of constant contact in football and allowed me to travel with a smaller, more intimate group. Though tied to competition, these trips felt like glimpses into a larger world I hadn't yet considered. I could take eight or more flights in two semesters without financially burdening my family. These opportunities planted seeds of curiosity and wonder within me, even if I didn't realize their full significance.

Chapter 4
Transcendence – Beyond the Field

How lessons from sports transcended the arena, influencing other aspects of life—relationships, leadership, resilience.

> **"The field taught me more about life than I ever imagined. This was my classroom for growth."**

Imagination as a Blueprint for Transformation

Imagination, a force not bound by the constraints of reality, is the ultimate tool for envisioning possibilities that have yet to exist. It allows us to step outside our current circumstances and design a future shaped by our desires and aspirations. While memory reflects what has been, imagination projects what could be. This forward-thinking ability to visualize potential outcomes is a powerful motivator, aligning our energy and actions with the life we wish to create.

The more time I spent on campus and in the surrounding community, the disparity in quality of life compared to where I came from became increasingly apparent. On the surface, the environments weren't drastically different, but the energy felt distinctly altered. I'm sure part of that was tied to the fact that I was an athlete—a role that came with a certain level of coddling and access because, as an athlete, you are viewed as an investment.

However, the community that raised me in many cases was viewed as a liability by society, a perception that I found deeply unjust. I was figuring out how those two opposing but significant identities could dwell in one constantly evolving mind. This period of my life demanded a deep reflection and caused those internal emotional tectonic plates to shift around my identity as a person of African descent in America.

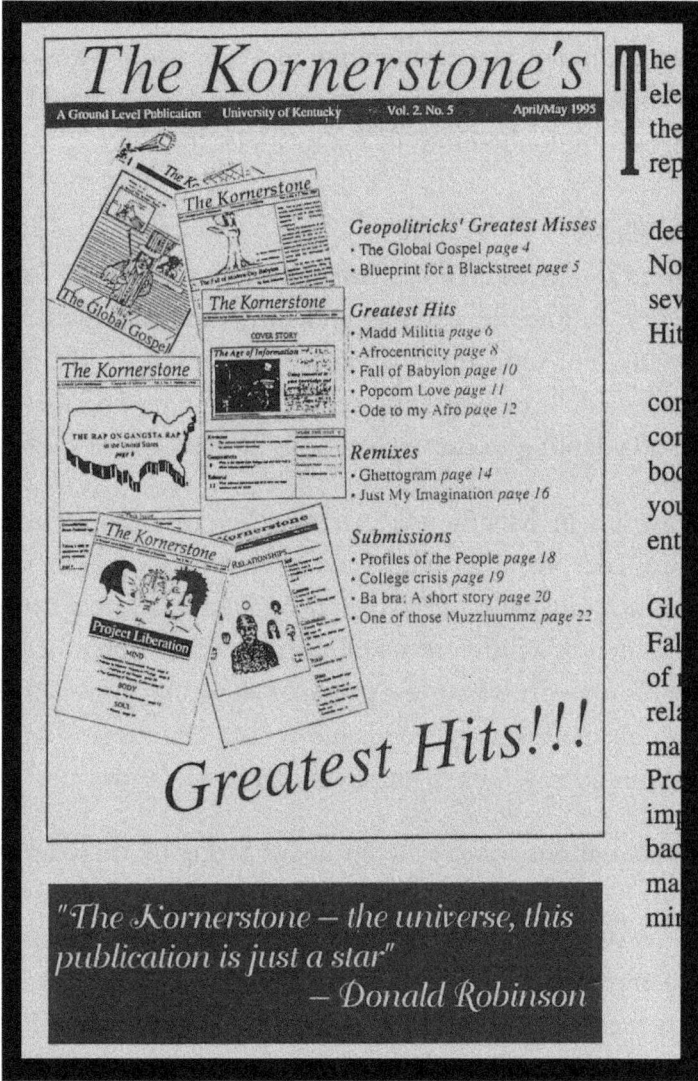

I was born and raised in the capital of the former confederacy - Richmond, Virginia - and had questions, opinions, and assumptions I needed to address. The process of crystallizing my identity and experience through creative writing was not just a means of making it visible to the campus and the broader community but a powerful tool for self-expression. It was a way to share my unique perspective with the world, a testament to the transformative power of words. Perhaps these actions were a response to an unconscious fear of losing a part of myself in this predominantly white environment. I'm unsure if that was the case, but I understand how a sudden change that moves you into a drastically different environment can impact your person. An environment that didn't look to change but looked toward me to adjust to fit in.

The Avatar Shahid

The dynamics at play when dominant cultures import talent from seemingly "inferior" cultures are complex and deeply rooted in power, identity, and belonging. For individuals navigating these spaces, the experience often involves a delicate balancing act between preserving their authentic selves and adapting to the expectations of a foreign ecosystem.

Growing up in Richmond's African American communities, my identity was deeply intertwined with that environment's cultural rhythms, values, and collective experiences. Stepping into a new cultural space dominated by a different set of norms and hierarchies triggered an instinctive response. It wasn't just a mental adjustment but a physiological one. My awareness heightened, and speech and expression emerged as unconscious adaptations to an unfamiliar social landscape.

These adaptations weren't merely about fitting in; they were survival mechanisms, ways to navigate a system that often subtly (or overtly) reinforces its dominance. While valuing the talent and perspectives of individuals from marginalized backgrounds, the dominant culture usually expects them to conform to its norms, leaving little room for the full expression of their cultural identity. This creates a tension between the individual's need to belong and their desire to remain true to themselves.

For me, this tension manifested as a fear of losing a part of myself—a fear that my cultural rhythm, so integral to my identity, might be drowned out by this new environment's louder, more dominant pulse. It wasn't just about adapting to new rules; it was about negotiating the unspoken power dynamics that dictate who gets to set those rules and who must follow them.

In this context, the act of importing talent from "inferior" cultures is not neutral. It carries with it an implicit expectation of assimilation, often at the expense of the individual's cultural authenticity. For the individual, the challenge lies in finding a way to thrive without erasing the very identity that makes them unique. It's a dance between adaptation and preservation, one that requires both resilience and a deep understanding of the dynamics at play.

Richmond Afro 1968

From the editor's desk...

By Donald Robinson

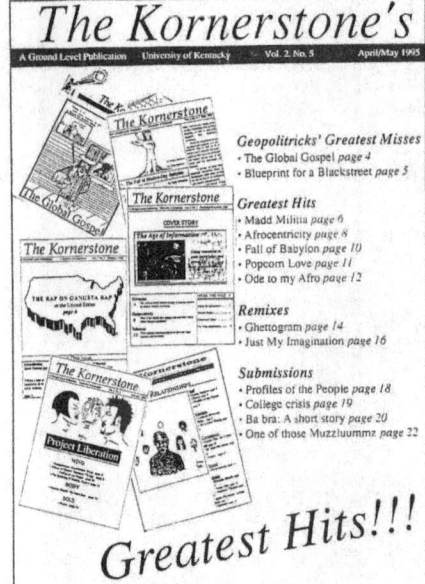

"The Kornerstone — the universe, this publication is just a star"
— Donald Robinson

The seventh sun of *The Kornerstone* electrifies a new horizon. Each issue of the publication leads up to this issue, representing a millenium.

Before this moment, you stood six deep in the waters of *The Kornerstone*. Now observe, as we ressurect into the seventh issue, "Kornerstone's Greatest Hits."

Together we will witness a new consciousness coming forth, a God consciouness. New and improved bodies of work will shine down upon your mind and heart, providing nutrients for those internal seeds of justice.

A constructive journey through the Global Gospels informs us about the Fall of Babylon, on through chambers of respect in the world of hip-hop, relating, and living in the age of information — until we organized for Project Liberation, discussing the importance of relationships. So, sit back and observe as these individual masons build and destroy you into a mindstate called Freedom.

At that time, I was not fully cognizant of this dynamic. I was living in the moment, fully immersed in the expressive freedoms of my late teens and early twenties. Looking back, the Kornerstone newsletter was not just a project but a personal journey that symbolized my transformation: At 19, I stood at the crossroads of two worlds: the one I was born into and the one I chose to create. This was not just a step forward but a weighty shift in perspective, a rebirth akin to the rhythm of nature itself. It felt as though the universe, in its infinite cycles of creation and renewal, had aligned to show me that transformation is inevitable when we align ourselves with purpose. My journey to campus was more than a geographical move—it was a spiritual one. It was as if I was shedding an old skin, stepping into a life not defined by the past but actively crafted by my vision of the future, a future that I eagerly anticipated.

This transformation echoed a story close to my heart: my father's. At just 20, with the birth of his first son, he too experienced a rebirth—a moment that demanded he rise to the challenge of fatherhood, of manhood. My rebirth, though different in form, carried the same essence. It was a moment to redefine what it means to live, to be present, and to create meaning in the face of challenges. This cyclical rebirth—father to son, generation to generation—symbolizes a universal truth: we are part of a greater design. Just as the seasons turn, stars are born, and rivers carve paths through mountains, we, too, have the power to transcend, transform, and shape a new reality for ourselves and those who come after us. The Kornerstone was a platform for raising awareness around the experiences, opinions, and contributions of people of color on campus.

OG Lessons in Vegas From Moe, Hotdog, and Blue.

This contrast between my identity and the new campus environment I was navigating continued to shape my mindset and outlook. I expressed myself freely, projected my growing sense of identity into the wider world, and wrestled with questions of justice and opportunity. My father, however, became concerned. He worried that my anger at the injustices I witnessed might lead me to make rash decisions after leaving university.

Living in another country for the first time is not just a change of scenery, but a profound journey of personal growth and transformation of perspective. In a place where no one knows your history, you're free to rediscover who you are. I found myself reflecting on the journeys of African American visionaries, those whose brilliance was embraced abroad even as their truths were dismissed at home.

Everything felt magnified: the weight of my talent, the privilege of being here, and the profound responsibility to represent not just myself but everyone who had contributed to my journey. Each day brought a small revelation—a new rhythm, a new culture, a new way of seeing the world.

Thankfully, I found my way into the Canadian Football League, which was a bridge to the next phase of my life. Looking back, I realize this transition allowed me to continue my love for travel. Although I wasn't consciously seeking out travel, my heart was deeply drawn to the freedom and excitement of new experiences it offered. After university, my first athletic journey led me to Las Vegas as part of my Canadian football career. The semester ended around May, and I was in Vegas by August. It was a different experience from Lexington, Ky., Unburdened by tangible responsibilities. The football camp housing in Las Vegas was at the Riviera Hotel, located on the Vegas Strip during the mid-1990s. This phase of my life allowed me to keep exploring the world and provided the time and space to look into my inner world through writing and self-expression.

Reading George GM James and John Henric Clarke's books about my ancient ancestors' extraordinary accomplishments gave me confidence and pride. No matter how strange or unfamiliar life became, I realized there is a power within me to access if I want to succeed and shine. After leaving campus to work in Vegas, I needed that extra support to enter the unknown.

As a teenager, my imagination was my escape and my teacher. I read books, and through their characters' eyes, I felt a deep connection and understanding, painting vivid pictures of places I'd never seen. I imagined the vibrant life Ali experienced in Africa and the intense transformation Malcolm found on his pilgrimage to Mecca. Watching Johnny Quest on TV, I marveled at the adventures in exotic locales, wondering how walking in those distant lands might feel. Canada, I thought, must be extraordinary, for Harriet Tubman risked her life to lead so many there away from the chains of slavery. After a season in Las Vegas, I ended up in Hamilton, Ontario.

My brief stint in a poetry class at McMaster University was a turning point. In that intimate group of eight, I shared my thoughts and verses, and to my surprise, they were met with genuine appreciation. It

The National Library of Poetry

11419-10 Cronridge Drive • Post Office Box 704 • Owings Mills, Maryland 21117 • (410) 356-2000

Wonderful verse
Select for "The Sound of Poetry"
CS

November 15, 1993

▮

Re: <u>Tears of Fire</u>

This publisher's proof represents your poem as it is now scheduled to appear in print. Please carefully review the publisher's proof . . . check carefully for typographical errors . . . indicate any changes directly on the proof, and return it to us in the enclosed envelope. If your poem is correct as is, please initial the proof, and return it without changes. <u>Please note that you must certify the accuracy of this proof by making appropriate changes.</u> ONLY INITIAL THE PROOF IF EVERYTHING IS CORRECT.

Lonely Travels

I guess I will spend my later days thinking about the sacrifice
of the son of God
the rising of the sun bares witness to the resurrection of the
living God and as the sun rises my consciousness will do the
same as the water flow, my soul will do the same, so now I sit
less than 100 years from my grave observing a life of vanity
serious thoughts over-populate my brain frame, do I truly
understand the significance of the sacrifice of the son of God?
I am a lost child of the cosmos searching for my home, there is
no more youth in these days, I feel the sun shining down on my
earthly body, encouraging a migration of my soul, then I sit in
darkness hiding from the illuminating lies of the beast
the sun is going down and the noises of the heathens are
growing I must focus on the sacrifice of the son of God, I will
search for the doctrine of the natural mystics and dance to the
rhythm of the birds, searching for a path that will lead into
the hypnotic mind state that shall send me to the land of my
ancestors forever

—Donald Robinson

Please return this proof within ~~one week~~ *4 weeks* so we can make our scheduled publication date.

* Poems must be 20 lines or less. Only one entry accepted per contestant.

x248x24

© The National Library of Poetry, 1992

was a moment of validation, a realization that my ideas could resonate with people beyond the borders of the United States. I couldn't help but reflect on the experiences of African American visionaries and authors I had read about—how they were often celebrated abroad, even when their messages were rejected at home. I could only imagine the sense of liberation and pride they must have felt, being recognized in ways that transcended national boundaries.

In that poetry class in 1996, I experienced a rare and profound sense of belonging. My voice and my words mattered in ways that made me question what I'd always accepted about identity and value. It became clear that crossing borders wasn't just physical; it was an emotional and spiritual journey, a liberation from narratives that had confined me.

This phase of my life was a journey of exploration. It allowed me to keep exploring the world and provided the time and space to look into my inner world through writing and self-expression. It was a time of curiosity and introspection, a time to understand myself and the world around me.

Love at Home

But before my experience of sharing my poetry at McMaster University, Alfafa's restaurant was across the street from the business college on the University of Kentucky's campus. It was there I did my first poetry reading. Standing before an all-white audience, I unleashed every militant phrase and black revolutionary idea I could recall from the books I had devoured. To my surprise, they showed me love—not because they fully understood my experience, but because they respected the rawness and truth of my words. That night, I learned something invaluable: even when perspectives clash, the power of shared humanity can bridge divides.

Imagination has always been my quiet force, guiding me toward new experiences and possibilities. From dreaming of faraway lands to standing before audiences, I began to see that the life I was imagining was already unfolding. The modern college experience, much like life itself, is a testing ground—a place to incubate ideas, challenge norms, and evolve. Through each poetic reading, shared thought, and brave leap into the unknown, I discovered the truth of personal evolution: it begins in the mind but grows through the courage to imagine and create. Even then, I realized that beauty is subjective, shaped by history, perspective, and the heart of the beholder.

Chapter 5
The Soul of an Athlete

"Echoes in the Stadium"(the lasting impact of moments on the field) Standing, Reflection, deep concentration. The final count. The ultimate push. The NOW. This is when I shine. It's loud but this internal voice is louder. 10 seconds from now, it will all be over. It's a win if I can carry what I feel right into the next moment. The momentum will be significant to me. It will embrace me. It will allow me to capture the energy from the Echoes in the Stadium. Store the energy until it bursts through my instincts and outshines my opponent. It's possible because I'm in a zone.

I'm a master. A zen master locked into a mission. The noise won't distract me from the wish fulfilled. I see it. The future is now. Right now. 10, 9,8,7,6,5,4,3,2,1 – I come to my senses and fully hear the Echoes in the Stadium. My teammates walked up to me and congratulated me on the play. I pause and fall back into a moment unaware of the noise as I consume the energy and fade into the Echos in the Stadium.

Echoes in the Stadium
I'm a master.
A zen master locked into a mission,
where focus sharpens like a blade of light,
cutting through the noise, the doubt, the chatter.
What only matters is my ability to change matter into what really matters to me
It is part of my athletic pedigree
A higher state born from my experiences in ghetto alchemy

It is part of my pedigree. A higher state born from my experiences in ghetto alchemy. Changing the state of negativity into positive expressions of athletic symmetry.

Player PICK OF THE WEEK

Hamilton Tiger-Cats

Number: #9
Name: Don Robinson
Position: CB

Name: Don Robinson
Height: 6'0"
Weight: 190
Born: May 27/72 - Richmond, Virginia
College: University of Kentucky
Wife's name: -N-
Children: -N-
Favorite Movie: Clear and Present Danger
Favorite TV Show: New York Undercover
Favorite Type of Music: Crazy Vershile
Favorite Recording Artists: Bob Marley, KRS One, and Sack
Favorite Pre-Game Meal: Pasta and Chicken
Favorite Pro Sports Team (other than the Tiger-Cats): None
Childhood Hero: Pops
What did you do this past off-season: Worked out, received subsidy amount from Dorrance Publishing Company
Career Highlight: Playing against the Florida Gators in 1991, 2 interceptions and 8 solo tackles
Name three people, living or dead, you would like to meet: Hannibal, Queen of Sheba, Jesus Christ
After your football career is over, what would you like to do: Travel, get money.

Photos by John Sokolowski/JOGO Inc.

THE GREATEST SHOW ON TURF!

Changing the state of negativity into positive expressions of athletic symmetry

Tapping into my opponents genealogy
downloading information about his movement preference
aggressive, dominant tendencies.
I would dive deeper during workouts
reflecting on breath control, mind control, arm leg, leg worshiped
visualizing the end, feeding myself calculated mind prophecies until the present blends
to the wish fulfilled and do it all over again.

The wish fulfilled whispers softly in my mind.
I see it—clear, unwavering.
The future is not a distant shore.
It's now.
Right now.
10, 9, 8…
The countdown hums,
like a drumbeat anchoring the soul.
7, 6, 5…
Every breath, a step closer to destiny.
4, 3, 2, 1…
I come to my senses,
a moment of clarity bursting like sunlight through clouds.
I hear it. The echoes.
The stadium reverberates with energy,
not just of sound, but of belief,
a symphony of purpose aligning with fate.

My teammates surround me,
their congratulations falling like raindrops
on the surface of my awareness.
And yet, I pause.
The noise fades to the periphery.
I consume the energy,
its power coursing through me like electric currents,
weaving the threads of past and present into a single ministry.
And then, I fade.
Not into the noise,
but into the echoes—
a place beyond sound and silence,
where the roar of the crowd
meets the quiet resolve of the soul.
There, in the Echoes of the Stadium,
I am whole.

Chapter 6
Football Expanded My World View

"Echoes in the Stadium"(the lasting impact of moments on the field)
Traveling is a transformative journey, akin to entering a new arena. While the fundamental principles may be the same, the differing environments challenge us to adapt and grow. Just as athletes train in various conditions to prepare for any situation, visiting new places reshapes our perspectives. Our experiences and insights serve as invaluable coaches, revealing what we may have overlooked and broadening the way we see the world. Each destination acts as a practice drill, and every encounter provides a lesson, collectively helping us redefine our approach to the game of life.

I stood in the Barcelona airport, mesmerized by the visions around me. In 1997, the terminal walls were adorned with artwork reflecting African culture—bold, beautiful, and unapologetic. At the time, I assumed it was a depiction of the Moors coming ashore in Spain. I couldn't understand how they felt so free to showcase this part of African history for the world to see. It was both inspiring and unfamiliar, like witnessing a truth I had always known but never fully seen celebrated. I imagined how it would feel to bask in the full expression of an African legacy, displayed openly for all to admire. That thought lingered with me even as I stepped outside the airport. The sunlight seemed to shine differently, more brightly, as if the world itself was illuminated by something more profound.

Sitges was breathtaking. The music, like an unspoken soundtrack, added electricity to every moment. Perfect weather, radiant sunlight, effortless fashion, and the energy of the beach all left an indelible mark

I walked in with my teammates, and the music was blaring as the bar glowed with fluorescent lights. It was our first day off in weeks, and I craved an experience with a familiar face. I spotted a dark brown Asian woman with braids standing with friends, so I approached her and asked where she was from.

Moments later, I invited her to meet me in Barcelona the next day to show me around. Twenty-five years later, we are the best of friends. I took a chance following my instinct and desire for a new experience. This relationship has taught me that reciprocity, authenticity, passion, and imagination can make dreams come true.

on my memory. Just four years earlier, I had been finishing my last season at the University of Kentucky, completely unaware of how much my worldview was about to expand and change again. Who could have imagined it? An eight-year-old African American kid from Church Hill, growing up playing Pop Warner football, is now spending a summer in Spain playing American football and traveling across Europe for games. The journey felt like a dream, a testament to life's unexpected paths.

I had experiences that changed my life and my perspective on the world. Every day, my teammates and I walked past a topless beach on our way to the bus for practice. While I wasn't particularly excited about the practice, I looked forward to walking by the beach. During that time, I bought a two-CD set of Nina Simone's music, which included my favorite song "Plain Gold Ring." Before traveling to Spain, I had never purchased any of Nina Simone's music. I envisioned meeting some great artists in person, and to my surprise, I met Nina on a double CD by chance, walking around Sitges one afternoon with no intention of buying any music. Her voice was just as beautiful as I had imagined, and I listened to "Plain Gold Ring" repeatedly.

Also, I bought a Wu-Tang CD at the airport after returning from a game. After exiting the plane, we went to a dance club in Barcelona that evening. Nobody in the club spoke English, but I handed the DJ my CD, and he started playing Wu-Tang tracks. This was in 1997, and what's funny is I had imagined being in a club listening to Wu-Tang banging through the speakers, which then manifested when I was in that club in Spain. I kept imagining how good it could get, and then I celebrated by drinking champagne after winning the NFL Europe championship weeks later.

Years later, I finally understood why the sunlight seemed different each morning—it wasn't the light that changed; it was me. Life, like sports, alters your perspective with every win, loss, and adjustment. As a seasoned player learns to read the game differently with experience, I realized that the light reflected my evolving perception, shaped by the revelations and travels of my journey. The field doesn't change; the player does. And with every step forward, the world becomes richer, deeper, and more meaningful, offering new opportunities to score in ways once unimaginable.

Traditional ideas of masculinity

In the 1990s, the archetype of the alpha male football player was firmly rooted in strength, dominance, and an unspoken adherence to traditional ideas of masculinity. On the field, this meant displays of physical power and unwavering confidence. Off the field, it often translated into suppressing vulnerability or anything perceived as softness. To step into the realm of poetry—a domain that thrives on introspection, emotion, and sensitivity—was, for many, an act that challenged the status quo. And to write lines about the sensuality of a woman, attempting to capture their essence not through conquest but through reverence, admiration, and awe, was an even more significant deviation from the script.

The internal struggle between my true self and the person I aspired to be was a battle I couldn't ignore. To quiet the noise, I sometimes lived recklessly, making decisions that felt like breaking the rules. But these so-called mistakes weren't failures; they were like practice matches—rough, unpolished, but full of lessons. Each misstep was an opportunity to see myself beyond the rigid framework of expectations. The daring moves weren't about rebelling against family values, but about finding space to redefine them. I began to understand that growth doesn't happen within the boundaries of a set play; it happens in the moments when you step off the script and face the unknown.

These experiences led me to a deep realization: the persona I excelled at was not a prison, but a launchpad. Family values were never intended to be shackles; they were roots, anchoring me as I strived for my own dreams. The mistakes I made and the lessons I learned were not deviations from my family's vision—they were extensions of it. Just as a seasoned athlete combines both training and instinct to excel, I found a way to respect the legacy I inherited while embracing the freedom to define myself. It's not about discarding the rulebook, but about crafting new strategies, ones that resonate with both the values I inherited and the person I've evolved into.

For an alpha male football player to pen such verses in the 1990s was an act of quiet rebellion, a subversion of the rigid constructs of masculinity. At a time when expressing sensitivity might provoke questions about one's manhood, writing poetry about a woman's sensuality was more than an artistic endeavor; it was a risk. Yet, within this act lay a penetrating assertion of identity—a resolute refusal to be confined by stereotypes. It demonstrated that strength is not diminished by vulnerability but rather enhanced by the courage to embrace it. In this context, the juxtaposition of brawn and lyricism becomes a testament to the complexity of humanity, showing that even those cast as symbols of unyielding masculinity are capable of tenderness, introspection, and the appreciation of beauty in its most unadulterated form.

It was like a scene from Robert Anton Wilson's book forcing me to rethink what I thought I knew about females through the lens of my experience as an athlete, a moment that forever shifted my perception of power, intimacy, and autonomy.

She invited me over that day after practice, casual in her demeanor yet with an undercurrent of purpose that I couldn't quite place. I followed her upstairs in silence, my curiosity growing with each step. As we entered her room, the sunlight pierced through the window, bathing the space in golden hues. The late afternoon light seemed to heighten everything—the colors, the shadows, and the quiet charge of her presence.

She didn't speak much, nor did she need to. Something in the way she moved, deliberate and unhurried, commanded attention. I stood there, uncertain of what was unfolding, when she began to undress. Her actions were not for my benefit, not a performance or a plea for approval. She was utterly self-contained, a woman stepping into her own space of power.

Then, without a glance in my direction, she laid across her bed and began to please herself. It was an intimate and raw act, yet it had nothing to do with me. I stood there, transfixed—not aroused, not diminished, but deeply humbled. I saw a woman in her full power of sensuality, creating her ecstasy without the need for anyone else participation.

Until then, we hadn't been lovers and wouldn't become lovers that evening. She wasn't inviting me to join her; she wasn't asking for anything. She simply wanted me present. It was as if my role was to bear witness, to see her not as a reflection of my desires but as a sovereign capable of creating and sustaining her joy.

In that moment, something transformed within me. The dynamic between men and women, desire and power, presence and purpose, took a new shape. I had always believed strength was something visible, something exerted or claimed. But here, in her unapologetic vulnerability, I saw strength in its most insightful form: the ability to own oneself completely without apology or permission. That evening revealed something to me that no Kama Sutra, film, or philosophy ever could in my early 20s: women hold within them a deep well of power—a divine force of creation that exists entirely on its own, independent of anyone else.

Chapter 7
Critiqued Poems

The Critique

Finding these marked-up pages while cleaning out a storage chest sparked something in me. This unexpected discovery became the catalyst for bringing this entire project to life, and I'm excited to see what these old words might reveal through fresh eyes. These are the poems from my 2001 creative writing class critique, initially written in the early 1990s. I can't recall why these specific poems were chosen for review, but I'm thrilled to revisit these pieces and share the insights they're about to reveal—both about my younger self and the creative journey that followed.

Before likes, retweets, or reposts, there was only paper—a tangible space where words lived, raw and unfiltered. Each poem was a universe unto itself, ink pressed into the fibers of a page, waiting for someone to enter and leave their mark. Feedback wasn't instantaneous or fleeting; it required deliberate engagement. One had to pick up a pen physically, summon one's thoughts, and invest energy into transcribing one's emotions. Praise, critique, and response were deeply personal, written with the weight of sincerity and the permanence of the medium. Every comment carried the writer's voice—an unspoken dialogue etched alongside the poem, creating a layered narrative where the original work and the reactions intertwined.

This collection comes from a pre-social media era where every mark on the paper was imbued with meaning. These poems were born of quiet reflection and read in still moments passed hand to hand among a small circle of kindred spirits. Their margins became a forum, a testament to the power of shared thought. The words of other writers remain here, scribbled critiques, underlined stanzas, or occasional bursts of enthusiasm scrawled boldly in the corners. Together, these artifacts tell a story of creation and connection—of a time when responses were not measured by algorithms but by the sincerity of human touch.

Fantasy

Introduction to poem: I guess nothing is lonelier than pieces of a distant love reality twisted and drenched into love fantasy.

Sub-introduction: Love fantasy

Pre-eminent energy vibrated from her outer contour, smooth and affectionate.
The remnants of her smile are jewels scattered across the shores of my mind.
Her voice gently caresses my ears as her words slowly disappear into the deserted chambers of a love thirsty mind.
Her skin glows like a fine brown silk
She eases her hand across my face neutralizing the tension with a healing touch
I cruise over feminine waters until I sink into a coma of wishful thinking
Soul searching within a cosmic paradise for her womanish fancies
Her love is exotic because it dances effortlessly and nude until my hormones give a standing ovation
Men can hunt me down and capture my wealth
However
Never will they be able to separate me from my true treasure
My infinite pleasure
She is my wisdom tree
Deep rooted in my love fantasy

Don Robinson

is there a title?

Introduction to poem: I guess nothing is lonelier than pieces of a distant love reality twisted and drenched into love fantasy.

Sub-introduction: Love fantasy

I don't get the necessity.? Help? for a "sub-introduction"

Pre-eminent energy vibrated from her outer contour, smooth and affectionate.

The remnants of her smile are jewels scattered across the shores of my mind.

Her voice gently caresses my ears as her words slowly disappear into the deserted *cliché*

chambers of a love thirsty mind

Her skin glows like a fine brown silk

She eases her hand across my face neutralizing the tension with a healing touch
nice *word feels too big?*
I cruise over feminine waters until I sink into a coma of wishful thinking *ok you*

Soul searching within a cosmic paradise for her womanish fancies

Her love is exotic because it dances effortlessly and nude until my hormones give a
don't want you to have this — want you to describe this — standing ovation *this is crafty.*

Men can hunt me down and capture my wealth

However *but*

Never ~~will they be able to separate~~ me from my true treasure
could they keep

My infinite pleasure —— *cliché*

~~She is~~ my wisdom tree

Deep rooted in my love fantasy

Don Robinson

Don, sometimes your words are all powerful AND all yours — sometimes they are overused and too easy. sometimes I think you try too hard to break out of "typical patterns" AND don't try hard enough to establish your own unique voice. You have a great deal of passion for poetry but you don't seem to have a lot of interest in exploring other ways of saying things poetically? what happened to your mid-term...?

48 • Athletic Alchemy

[handwritten at top, bracketing the introduction:] The way you introduce the beginning is very original

[handwritten at top right:] But the loneliness which you speak of is not found in the rest of the poem

Introduction to poem: ~~I guess~~ Nothing is lonelier than pieces of a distant love reality twisted and drenched into love fantasy.

Sub-introduction: Love fantasy

Pre-eminent energy vibrated from her outer contour, smooth and affectionate.

★The remnants of her smile are jewels scattered across the shores of my mind.

Her voice gently caresses my ears as her words slowly disappear into the deserted chambers of a love thirsty mind

Her skin glows like a fine brown silk   *→ I suppose this does sound a bit clinical*

★She eases her hand across my face neutralizing the tension with a healing touch

★I cruise over feminine waters until I sink into a coma of wishful thinking

★Soul searching within a cosmic paradise for her womanish fancies

Her love is exotic because it dances effortlessly and nude until my hormones give a standing ovation   *(H.P.M)*

Men can hunt me down and capture my wealth   *) ? Seems kind of thrown in here to me*

However

Never will they be able to separate me from my true treasure

My infinite pleasure

<u>She is my wisdom tree</u>

<u>Deep rooted in my love fantasy</u>

Don Robinson

I like the idea of "conclusion"

[handwritten at left margin:] The way you express sexual feeling works very well.

Beautiful poem.

Introduction to poem: I guess nothing is lonelier than pieces of a distant love reality twisted and drenched into love fantasy.

Sub-introduction: **Love fantasy**

⟨Pre-eminent energy vibrated from her outer contour, smooth and affectionate.⟩
The remnants of her smile are jewels scattered across the shores of my mind.
Her voice gently caresses my ears as her words slowly disappear into the deserted
chambers of a love thirsty mind
Her skin glows like a fine brown silk
She eases her hand across my face neutralizing the tension with a healing touch
I cruise over feminine waters until I sink into a coma of wishful thinking
Soul searching within a cosmic paradise for her womanish fancies
Her love is exotic because it dances effortlessly and nude until my hormones give a
standing ovation
Men can hunt me down and capture my wealth
However
Never will they be able to separate me from my true treasure
My infinite pleasure
She is my wisdom tree
Deep rooted in my love fantasy

Don Robinson

try to go inside this and talk about it — it could be a part of this or a whole new poem

I dig this

Introduction to poem: I guess nothing is lonelier than pieces of a distant love-reality twisted and drenched into love fantasy.

Sub-introduction: Love fantasy

try to take out some of the prepositions

Us & The
Body.
I

Pre-eminent energy vibrated from her outer contour, smooth and affectionate.
The remnants of her smile are jewels scattered across the shores of my mind.
Her voice gently caresses my ears as her words ~~slowly~~ disappear into the ~~deserted~~ *empty* chambers of a love thirsty mind.
Her skin glows like a fine brown silk.

make repetit?

II

She eases her hand across my face neutralizing the tension with a healing touch
I cruise over feminine waters until I sink into a coma of wishful thinking
Soul searching within a cosmic paradise for her womanish fancies
Her love is exotic because it dances effortlessly and nude until my hormones give a standing ovation

Men can hunt me down and capture my wealth
However
Never will they be able to separate me from my true treasure
My infinite pleasure
She is my wisdom tree
Deep rooted in my love fantasy

III
Conclusion.
I like it

Don Robinson

go farther keep reaching — *I love the 3rd part the most*

- think about the format of this poem
  do you want it in the center? It slightly distracts for line breaks
  — This could easily read as a prose poem
  — or in stanzas
  — or down the side just like this ——— don't be afraid to play w/ this

Thank you ▮▮▮▮
Thank you
you rock

Look

> Look hard enough and...

Enter the realms of mental stamina and discover new un-authorized territories of mind control. Un-attended minds wilt like lifeless trees because they lack the fortified culture needed to nurture their roots and neutralize negativity. The mind is the supreme explorer shedding light on the path of those individuals with injured realities looking to be healed by ultimate truth. Citizens are hypnotized by madness and breast-fed violence so no one is surprised when supervised massacres become a reality. Society has fallen short of truth and grown too tall for justice. Behold when intelligent tongues speak forcing wickedness back into its tomb of destruction. Ignorance skinny-dips in the rivers of society feeling no shame for his vulgar actions because barbarians justifies his motives and awards him with the trophy of ethnocide. The masses are easily relaxed by the slumberous words of elected hypocrites and the story goes on unless...

Don Robinson

[Marginalia: "nice"; "better analogy here"; "skinny-dips/vulgar"; "You have a strong voice"; "Flush Left"]

Don — I enjoy and appreciate the ideas you're expressing here. I think it would be a neat idea to try and format this in a "flushed-left" poetic style... it might be easier to read b/c there's so much here. Try a different title to pull your reader in. I like the language and it's very "story-telling" tone.

52 • Athletic Alchemy

Handwritten top right: Don't Listen to them.

Look hard enough and…

Enter the realms of mental stamina and discover new un-authorized territories of mind control. Un-attended minds wilt like lifeless trees because they lack the fortified culture needed to nurture their roots and neutralize negativity. The mind is the supreme explorer shedding light on the path of those individuals with injured realities looking to be healed by ultimate truth. Citizens are hypnotized by madness and breast-fed violence so no one is surprised when supervised massacres become a reality. Society has fallen short of truth and grown too tall for justice. Behold when intelligent tongues speak forcing wickedness back into its tomb of destruction. Ignorance skinny-dips in the rivers of society feeling no shame for his vulgar actions because barbarians justifies his motives and awards him with the trophy of ethnocide. The masses are easily relaxed by the slumberous words of elected hypocrites and the story goes on unless…

Don Robinson

Handwritten annotations:
- great, man
- tense agreement
- Are these 2 truths the same.
- This is very "Mos Def" meets "Jeru the Damaja" (That's a compliment for sure) KINDA Dead Prez, too.
- I don't know man, it has a voice, unlike the other poems. It's you and not some "Thought up you"
- I like the form.
- I like the speed.

Look hard enough and…

Enter the realms of mental stamina and discover new un-authorized territories of mind control. Un-attended minds wilt like lifeless trees because they lack the fortified culture needed to nurture their roots and neutralize negativity. The mind is the supreme explorer shedding light on the path of those individuals with injured realities looking to be healed by ultimate truth. Citizens are hypnotized by madness and breast-fed violence so no one is surprised when supervised massacres become a reality. Society has fallen short of truth and grown too tall for justice. Behold when intelligent tongues speak forcing wickedness back into its tomb of destruction. Ignorance skinny-dips in the rivers of society feeling no shame for his vulgar actions because barbarians justifies his motives and awards him with the trophy of ethnocide. The masses are easily relaxed by the slumberous words of elected hypocrites and the story goes on unless…

Don Robinson

Look hard enough and…

Enter the realms of mental stamina and discover new un-authorized territories of mind control. Un-attended minds wilt like lifeless trees ~~because they~~ lacking the fortified culture needed to nurture their roots and neutralize negativity. The mind is the supreme explorer shedding light on the path of those individuals with injured realities looking to be healed by ultimate truth. Citizens are hypnotized by madness and breast-fed violence so no one is surprised when supervised massacres become a reality. Society has fallen short of truth and grown too tall for justice. Behold when intelligent tongues speak forcing wickedness back into its tomb of destruction. Ignorance skinny-dips in the rivers of society feeling no shame for his vulgar actions because barbarians justifies his motives and awards him with the trophy of ethnocide. The masses are easily relaxed by the slumberous words of elected hypocrites and the story goes on unless…

Don Robinson

Margin annotations:

- Nice rhyme! Rhyme I like this word
- Nice word
- just maybe help (www) 2 or 3 of your images
- yes. yes.
- What you're writing is hard. and it should be. Thank you.
- Good. very strong.
- right word? i do like its sound, though
- I love the personification of intangibles in your poem. Ignorance skinny-dips! Damn. I love that.
- breast-fed violence — wow unexpected
- (Write the "unless…" poem.) you have such good words. Sound seems so important to you. i love the way this piece flows — one into the next. Nice!
- take some of this flow + sound and play w/ some very concrete images to like the images you see behind the words in your poem. (like the sight of kids screaming away from Columbine, etc.) i think you should play with form, but i like this style too — you have to write it for you first
- Joe i would love to talk pretty soon. This class is so powerful
- @ prodigy.net
- 10/10/01
- it's so
- Thank you for your poem so much for so important

Look hard enough and...

Enter the realms of mental stamina and discover new un-authorized territories of mind control. Un-attended minds will like lifeless trees because they lack the fortified culture needed to nurture their roots and neutralize negativity. The mind is the supreme explorer shedding light on the path of those individuals with injured realities looking to be healed by ultimate truth. Citizens are hypnotized by madness and breast-fed violence, no one is surprised when supervised massacres become a reality. Society has fallen short of truth and grown too tall for justice. Behold when intelligent tongues speak forcing wickedness back into its tomb of destruction. Ignorance skinny-dips in the rivers of society feeling no shame for his vulgar actions because barbarians justifies his motives and awards him with the trophy of ethnocide. The masses are easily relaxed by the slumberous words of elected hypocrites and the story goes on unless...

Don Robinson

[Handwritten annotations:]

You say such broad statements here. Maybe use some real examples, give specific images

I like how you trail off here

"It's very hard to read (for me) when it's in this structure. I made some slashes where you might make paragraph lines after sounds, to highlight certain words."

Personally, the form doesn't work for me. I feel like I'm rushed on to the next sentence before I (maybe, I'm just slow) can process the first. Also, I'm a really visually oriented person + this kind of format just doesn't catch my eye.

So much in this poem! Very revelatory, insightful. I think you need some things in this poem to slow it down — AND — I think it will be more powerful that way.

I love how your work is so accurate + unflinching when it comes to depicting society.

56 • Athletic Alchemy

My King

My King needs to Know

[handwritten: i love the repetition so good so good]
[handwritten: DO NOT CHANGE THE BEGINNING.]

Naturally the wind will blow *[handwritten: i really]*
Naturally the sun shall shine *[handwritten: will]*
So naturally *[handwritten: cry :)]*
I willingly enlist my deepest feelings of desire in the war for your kingdom
Just crown me the queen of your heart
My lips are like two dark thunder clouds parting after a violent storm bringing peace and inner tranquility
I will send my warriors two liberate you from the shackles of uncertainty
My king if you ever get stranded call upon me and my words will rescue you
Come into me and love my body
Study my mind and I shall quiz you on the grounds of forever
I am your wisdom chest
So search in me for your treasures
When you feel cold call upon the sun to shine down on you brow
For God is good
Look deep sweetheart and you will taste him in my smile
I am the feminine star that shines on your soft side
After the war come lay with me in the garden
And I will heal your wounds with pieces of paradise my love
Sprinkle me over your life
And I will make it feel so good my King
So good

Don Robinson

[handwritten right margin: i like all the lines / maybe not need end part]

[handwritten: i like it; its unexpected / you need not coddle the reader and spoon-feed them w/ what's easy. you work well w/ language]

[handwritten bottom: Oh my gosh i love this. This is my favorite piece. The sound and rhythmn is so awesome! The images are so vivid, they jump right up into the readers face, but with soft, sensual steps. i love that you write in a female voice. i think that's a definite tribute to your writing. i'd like a copy of this, please :) you are awesome!]

My King needs to Know [handwritten: beautiful title, but I'm not sure how they tie in with the poem?]

Naturally the wind will blow
Naturally the sun shall shine
So naturally
I willingly enlist my deepest feelings of desire in the war for your kingdom
Just crown me the queen of your heart
My lips are like two dark thunder clouds parting after a violent storm bringing peace and [handwritten: are your lips like the clouds or the clouds parting?]
inner tranquility
I will send my warriors to liberate you from the shackles of uncertainty [handwritten: too general, what is the "you" uncertain about?]
My king if you ever get stranded call upon me and my words will rescue you
Come into me and love my body [handwritten: too blunt, doesn't go together with the tenderness + imagery of the rest]
Study my mind and I shall quiz you on the grounds of forever
I am your wisdom chest
So search in me for your treasures
When you feel cold call upon the sun to shine down on you brow [handwritten: too repetitive, cliché]
For God is good
Look deep sweetheart and you will taste him in my smile
I am the feminine star that shines on your soft side
After the war come lay with me in the garden
And I will heal your wounds with pieces of paradise my love
Sprinkle me over your life
And I will make it feel so good my King
So good

Don Robinson

[handwritten: I like the courtship/war/monarchy imagery in here, as well as the way you juxtapose male/female voices; I especially like how you take on the feminine voice.]

My King needs to Know

Naturally the wind will blow
Naturally the sun shall shine
So naturally
I willingly enlist my deepest feelings of desire in the war for your kingdom
Just crown me the queen of your heart
My lips are like two dark thunder clouds parting after a violent storm bringing peace and inner tranquility
I will send my warriors two liberate you from the shackles of uncertainty
My king if you ever get stranded call upon me and my words will rescue you
Come into me and love my body
Study my mind and I shall ruin you on the grounds of forever
I am your wisdom chest
So search in me for your treasures
When you feel cold call upon the sun to shine down on you brow
For God is good
Look deep sweetheart and you will taste him in my smile
I am the feminine star that shines on your soft side
After the war come lay with me in the garden
And I will heal your wounds with pieces of paradise my love
Sprinkle me over your life
And I will make it feel so good my King
So good

Don Robinson

My King needs to Know

Naturally the wind will blow
Naturally the sun shall shine
So naturally
I willingly enlist my deepest feelings of desire in the war for your kingdom *Kingdom being heart*
Just crown me the queen of your heart
My lips are like two dark thunder clouds parting after a violent storm bringing peace and inner tranquility
I will send my warriors ~~two~~ liberate you from the shackles of uncertainty
My king if you ever get stranded call upon me and my words will rescue you
Come into me and love my body
Study my mind and I shall quiz you on the grounds of forever
I am your wisdom chest *There might be a better metaphor for a place which holds knowledge less than wisdom chest. Something more accessable.*
So search in me for your treasures
When you feel cold call upon the sun to shine down on you brow
For God is good *what does God bring to this poem? It seems to be between a woman and a man. There this invokes marriage or a blessing of some kind*
Look deep sweetheart and you will taste him in my smile
I am the feminine star that shines on your soft side
After the war come lay with me in the garden
And I will heal your wounds with pieces of paradise my love
Sprinkle me over your life
And I will make it feel so good my King
So good

Don Robinson

I like some of the imagery and the force of seduction here. I think that the form takes away from it a little just because they carry so much in myth and make-up.

My King needs to Know

Naturally the wind will blow
Naturally the sun shall shine
So naturally
I willingly enlist my deepest feelings of desire in the war for your kingdom
Just crown me the queen of your heart
My lips are like two dark thunder clouds parting after a violent storm bringing peace and inner tranquility
I will send my warriors two liberate you from the shackles of uncertainty
My king if you ever get stranded call upon me and my words will rescue you
Come into me and love my body
Study my mind and I shall quiz you on the grounds of forever
I am your wisdom chest
So search in me for your treasures
When you feel cold call upon the sun to shine down on you brow
For God is good
Look deep sweetheart and you will taste him in my smile
I am the feminine star that shines on your soft side
After the war come lay with me in the garden
And I will heal your wounds with pieces of paradise my love
Sprinkle me over your life
And I will make it feel so good my King
So good

Don Robinson

My King needs to Know *[handwritten: Great title]*

Naturally the wind will blow
Naturally the sun shall shine *[handwritten: I like the use of intensity. Add a break here.]*
So naturally
I willingly enlist my deepest feelings of desire in the war for your kingdom
Just crown me the queen of your heart
My lips are like two dark thunder clouds parting after a violent storm bringing peace and inner tranquility
I will send my warriors to liberate you from the shackles of uncertainty *[handwritten: like use of uncertainty]*
My king if you ever get stranded call upon me and my words will rescue you
Come into me and love my body
Study my mind and I shall quiz you on the grounds of forever
I am your wisdom chest
So search in me for your treasures
When you feel cold call upon the sun to shine down on you brow
For God is good *[handwritten: Too cliche]*
Look deep sweetheart and you will taste him in my smile *[handwritten: these two lines don't fit as well for me]*
I am the feminine star that shines on your soft side
After the war come lay with me in the garden
And I will heal your wounds with pieces of paradise my love
Sprinkle me over your life
And I will make it feel so good my King
So good

Don Robinson

[handwritten left margin: I really like these — just not here. Love this part — sensual voice]

[handwritten bottom: Focus on Don's heart-felt words within his kind words. Don — As with your past pieces — give your strong voice & words a chance to breathe, seed, shine & illuminate our eyes like a candle — not like a raging forest fire.]

62 • Athletic Alchemy

Competitive Breathing: A Gateway to Wellness and Mindfulness

I didn't realize then that this conversation was my first introduction to wellness—a concept that would grow in depth and importance as I matured. Breathing is often taken for granted and dismissed as a subconscious act. Yet, intentional breath work is foundational to wellness and mindfulness practices. Controlled breathing supports physical stamina and regulates the mind, reducing stress and promoting clarity. My father's rhythmic breathing during his runs mirrored the principles of mindfulness: presence in the moment, awareness of the body, and intentionality in action. The simple act of breathing became a doorway into understanding the interconnectedness of mind and body—a principle central to athletic performance and holistic well-being.

Imagination, poetry, and sports. The tools I use to always redirect myself to the now, to the moment. Imagination was born from any moment I would visualize and create, and that's imagination. Poetry is the action, the outline, the container I use to add color and texture to transparent emotions, desires, and beliefs.

So, it was poetry, imagination, and sports. And sports was like the third level of physical manifestation. You know, the actual birthing of the initial energy, thought, or moment. Because even in poetry, I would capture a moment. I hone in 100 percent to the moment to reflect emotional depth in the poetry. It's similar to being present enough in the moment to knock away a pass right before the ball touches the receiver's fingers. Later, I replayed that play in my mind or watched the play in a film session each time, reliving the moment's emotions. I tried to freeze a feeling in its original energy state until I could describe it. It is the crystallized energy derived from the feelings and awareness of the moment.

And that's why I can read a poem 10 years or 20 years later, and it still has a life to it because the awareness I tapped into was realizing who I am in that moment, my relationship to a particular theme or idea, and how to process that realization and capturing it in that poem. Now, I see that everything is born from the power of the imagination.

My born day
The origin of An Earth Soldier Lifestyle
A Celebration in this picture. My second or third birthday within the richness of family and friends.

"Abject poverty refers to a state of extreme and severe poverty, characterized by a lack of basic necessities such as food, water, shelter, clothing, and healthcare.** It is often accompanied by poor living conditions, inadequate access to education and employment opportunities, and limited social and economic mobility."

GRANDMA CEO

On the field, this resilience manifests in every sprint, tackle, and play. But off the field, it is a call to honor their legacy by becoming more: more compassionate, more determined, and more attuned to the immense power within each of us.

Challenges test our will to survive, but they also ignite the fire to thrive. As athletes, we have the opportunity to let those experiences shape us into powerful instruments of change, creating harmony between personal growth and our impact on the world. True victory is living aligned with that purpose.

Some experiences help us determine what we don't want for ourselves or our loved ones. These experiences, at times, create the capacity in us to desire change from deep within. Sometimes, these experiences are life-changing and test our will to survive. When the reality of failed dreams or relationships boldly introduces itself in our lives, we can focus and survive with the power of gratitude. These experiences also serve as valuable lessons, enlightening and guiding our decisions.

When I found myself in Richmond touching down after having to separate from my children, a pivotal moment, I knew I had to wake up with a resolute mind, driven by a fierce determination to survive and thrive. I had to be grateful for the strength my faith in God restored in me. This was a lesson I had learned early in life- the art of 'wanting it more.' It's about the unwavering pursuit of our goals, even when the path is fraught with pain, discomfort, and doubt. It's about pushing through the challenges and never giving up, no matter how arduous the journey may seem.

Springers reach deep for victory

By Mike Hodge
News Leader sports writer

Highland Springs High showed why it is ranked No. 1 in Group AAA by The Associated Press.

Last night, the Springers beat cross-county rival Mills Godwin 20-13.

The Springers are a scrawny bunch. Only three starters weigh more than 200 pounds. They are beat up, hobbled from midseason bruises, sprains and strains to four key starters.

They won without linebacker Irving Carter and receiver David McLeod. Both missed the game because of sprained ankles. They won with Harry Wiles, a 145-pound nose guard who played with a bum hip and shoulder. They won with Chad Gillespie who played despite a nagging groin pull and scored the game's first points on an 82-yard punt return.

They won because they made the key plays, because they wouldn't give up, because they came together when they had to, because they stopped Godwin yards short of the tying points, because . . .

"Deep down, we wanted it more," Highland Springs' defensive back Donald Robinson said. "We're No. 1, and not many people have that much confidence in us. But the Springers wanted to prove that they are capable under pressure."

They did. After Highland Springs halfback Carl Smith fumbled at the

Springers' Donald Robinson: 'We wanted it more.'

I had to redeem myself, so I pulled myself together," Robinson said.

So did the Springers. Godwin (2-3) accounted for 14 first downs to Highland Springs' five and outgained the Springers 191 to 137.

So what happened?

"I thought we moved the ball well," Mills Godwin Coach Ron Axselle said. "But they moved it when they had to."

Highland Springs took three consecutive possessions before making a first down. The Springers had 84 yards rushing in the first half. Fifty of those came on one play, Smith's 50-yard touchdown run in the second

Chapter 8
The Arena – Lessons Learned Through Competition

The Community Raises You
The teenagers and 20-somethings were too young to communicate despair to me. These young people hadn't been fully hardened by a failed social justice system, even though they had every right to feel that way. They were just as excited about life as I was. With all their experiences, my grandmothers lived and mainly spoke to me with inspiration, always seeking opportunities to bring the family together and celebrate life, a joyous occasion that uplifts the spirit and fills the heart with joy. They knew I needed that upbringing because of the trauma I was born into. As a stamp of community approval, they gave me the name NewNew. Which is one of two nicknames that has stuck with me until this day. I was my maternal grandmother first grandchild. I had to symbolize something new and different from what my community was dealing with.

Its Parallels to African American Men
Whether art imitates life or life imitates art is as tricky as the chicken-and-egg analogy—each influences the other in ways that are often hard to untangle. This interplay becomes fascinating when examining how media reflects and perpetuates societal stereotypes. Take The Jason Bourne trilogy—a gripping action series. The films inadvertently mirror troubling stereotypes often associated with African American men, echoing real-world narratives that disproportionately frame Black men as threats or outsiders.

The Jason Bourne trilogy, consisting of "The Bourne Identity," "The Bourne Supremacy," and "The Bourne Ultimatum," is a popular action film series centered around the character of Jason Bourne, a highly skilled CIA operative suffering from memory loss – one of my favorite movies. While these movies have received acclaim for their thrilling action sequences and intense plots, a closer examination reveals certain problematic parallels between Jason Bourne's experiences and the stereotypes often associated with African American men.

Hyper-Violent Stereotypes:
Throughout the trilogy, Jason Bourne is portrayed as a highly skilled, hyper-violent character who resorts to aggressive tactics to survive and uncover the truth about his past. Unfortunately, this depiction aligns with long-standing stereotypes of African American men as violent and dangerous.

Criminalization of Black Identity:
In several instances, Jason Bourne is depicted as a fugitive, pursued by law enforcement agencies for actions he cannot remember. This portrayal mirrors the unfortunate reality faced by many African American men who are disproportionately targeted by law enforcement based on their race. A narrative of criminalization and racial profiling faced by African American men in society.

The Jason Bourne trilogy, with its exploration of identity and memory loss, presents a unique lens through which we can examine African Americans' broader societal struggles concerning cultural dislocation and identity. Bourne's struggle to reclaim his sense of self amidst institutional manipulation echoes the historical erasure of African American heritage through systemic oppression, slavery, and cultural assimilation.

Loss of Identity in African American Communities
For African Americans, the forced displacement from their native lands resulted in a severance from ancestral languages, customs, and cultural

practices. This erasure mirrors Bourne's amnesia: both experience an ongoing battle to piece together fragmented identities in environments designed to exploit their disorientation. Like Bourne, African Americans often navigate systems that obscure their heritage while demanding loyalty to structures that perpetuate inequities.

Impact on Personal and Cultural Identity
Just as Bourne struggles to decode cryptic clues to his past, African Americans grapple with a loss of linguistic and cultural ties. The lack of a shared ancestral language limits their ability to connect with their roots, creating a persistent void in their identity.

Cultural Misrepresentation:
Bourne's actions are often misunderstood or villainized by the institutions pursuing him, drawing parallels to how African Americans are stereotyped in American society. This misrepresentation fuels alienation and a distorted sense of self.

Fragmented Identity:
Bourne's fragmented memories compel him to question his role as both perpetrator and victim, reflecting how African Americans must reconcile pride in their resilience with the trauma of systemic oppression.

Just Be
I embodied that feeling of community and imagined having that experience again. I guess that's one of the reasons I was drawn to sports—the sense of community. My family in Richmond, a pillar of support, came together to win the game of life even though all perceived odds were stacked against us. Some of us sacrificed our bodies to get others across the line. Some of us got injured and removed from the game of life. Most of us kept playing with the memory of that person as inspiration to press forward. There were some good calls and plenty of bad ones.

How can I move the crowd?

The energy I often expressed on the basketball court, track field, and football field was not solely my own. It was a product of the support and nurturing I received from my community. Their intent was not to change me but to ensure I knew who I was. This technique of reflecting light, born from the energy source within, encouraged me and others in my community to discover and celebrate their sacred energy. When harnessed and shared, this personal energy becomes a powerful force that fuels community support and personal growth. I showed that light when I went into flow mode.

I'm confident that my grandmothers, too, slipped into flow mode when they shared their principles of celebration and belief in our family's survival. We were drawn to the light emanating from these messages. It was the understanding that within us lies the power and energy, a pearl of wisdom that my grandmothers used to sustain our community. Their wisdom, gained through years of experience, is a valuable resource that keeps us alive and thriving. In this sense, flow kept us alive while the flow on the field entertained the crowd as they watched me grow into a man while I transformed everyday lessons into magical acts on the field.

Community is the force that binds us, the shelter where we find strength when the odds seem insurmountable. Growing up in Richmond, my family embodied this spirit—a pillar of unwavering support, a team that came together not for trophies but for survival, justice, and dignity. I understand that not all communities have the same level of support, and we must work towards creating a more equitable society.

It's no wonder I was drawn to sports. On the field, I felt that same bond—a shared pursuit, a collective dream. Yet, I've seen that the game doesn't end when the whistle blows. The real challenge lies off the field, where the stakes are higher and the fight for equity and justice never rests. This fight is not just important, and it's urgent and significant.

The journey of rediscovering one's identity and legacy often involves peeling back layers of misinformation and confronting deeply ingrained beliefs. It is a process of reclaiming what was obscured and finding empowerment in the truths that were hidden. Within underserved communities, this act of rediscovery is not just personal—it is revolutionary. By honoring the principles and values passed down through generations, individuals can forge a path that both celebrates their roots and creates new possibilities for future generations.

This process of rediscovery also reveals a philosophical truth: culture is the immune system of a community. It protects against the erosion of identity and provides the framework for resilience in the face of adversity. When underserved communities reconnect with their cultural roots, they strengthen their collective defenses, fostering a sense of belonging, purpose, and continuity. Culture serves as a guide, a reminder of the values and principles that sustain life and enable progress. By nurturing and preserving this cultural wealth, individuals heal the wounds of the past and fortify themselves and their communities against future challenges.

What if the challenges reflected in the Bourne Trilogy weren't meant to break us but instead shape our destiny? The narratives that attempt to frame certain people as outsiders or threats may, in fact, be fueling an innate drive within us—a drive to compete, not just for survival, but to redefine the game entirely. Like the community of young people, including my parents who raised me, untouched by cynicism despite their circumstances, there is an unshaken resilience in those who refuse to be hardened by a failed system. They carry within them an energy, an excitement for life, and a silent but powerful determination to keep moving forward.

This interplay between perception and perseverance is crucial, especially when examining how media reinforces societal stereotypes. The Bourne Trilogy, for example, portrays a protagonist relentlessly pursued by forces beyond his control—an allegory that many can relate to. For generations, Black men have been depicted through a similar lens, cast as threats rather than as individuals navigating a system designed to limit their progress. And yet, what if the true lesson hidden within these narratives is that we are not merely meant to resist but to find a flow—a rhythm that allows us to exist beyond our expectations? To step outside survival mode and recognize that thriving itself is an act of defiance.

This resilience isn't accidental; it is inherited. My grandmothers, their siblings, and their community understood this deeply. They didn't just fight to survive—they strategized, adapted, and outlasted. Their survival was never about luck but an unspoken agreement, a collective understanding that giving up was not an option. They played the game not to endure but to rewrite the rules. In their eyes, hardship was not a barrier but a blueprint, a guide to navigating the world with intention and strength.

I am a descendant of this team, part of a lineage that chose perseverance over defeat. And I hope that those who see themselves in this story take the time to learn their history, to embrace their narrative, and to use it as a source of inspiration—both on the field and beyond. The system may have been designed for us to lose, but history shows that we are far too resilient to ever accept that outcome.

www.ingramcontent.com/pod-product-compliance
Lightning Source LLC
Chambersburg PA
CBHW032059150426
43194CB00006B/589